THE POWER OF HUMOR

Fr. Eugene Azorji

En Route Books and Media, LLC

Saint Louis, MO

USA

⊕ *ENROUTE*
Make the time

En Route Books and Media, LLC

5705 Rhodes Avenue

Saint Louis, MO 63109

Contact us at

contactus@enroutebooksandmedia.com

Cover credit: Sebastian Mahfood assisted by ChatGPT

Copyright: Eugene Azorji

ISBN-13: 979-8-88870-338-0

To Most Reverend Gregory Kelly, STD
(Bishop of Tyler, Texas).

His humility and compassion are amazing indeed!

May God bless his Episcopacy. Amen.

God has a sense of humor. In the creation narrative, he created human beings as adults not as kids, and he expected them to behave like adults, but unfortunately, they behaved like kids, and they were easily deceived by the evil one—the devil. He placed them in the garden of innocence, but they chose the garden of guilt. God asked them why they did what they did, and they began a blame game, which is consistent with worldly family way of life. "The woman you gave me did it," says the man, and "The serpent (you created) gave it to me, and I ate it," says the woman. They discovered they were naked when they strayed from the garden of innocence, but "who told you that you were naked?" So, the opening chapter of the bible begins with a sense of humor that is prevalent in the society even today.

Metaphor and humor can be very powerful tools of communication. There are varieties of communications. There are verbal and non-verbal communications. In both cases, humor and metaphor are essential. One can use for example, the facial expressions of smile, or sign language to communicate non-verbally. In African traditional families, couples communicate among themselves when they have visitors coming into the house. Humor and Metaphor can also be used verbally to keep the conversations going, and most importantly to extend the attention span of the audience in some situations.

In traditional African societies, humor and metaphor are types of genres that add flavor to the language of the people. Knowing the language is one thing, but when one uses humor and metaphor combined, that may be called an advanced acquisition of the language. The use of humor or metaphor is an expression of feelings from the deepest point of the human spirit, and it is a way to express and explain a narrative precisely.

As the saying goes, "When the eyes are blinded, the eyebrow will substitute to do what the eyes used to do." An elaborate explanation of this idiom indicates that the eyes are important, but when they fail to function, another part of the body can be used instead of the eye. It goes to illustrate that all parts of the body are important to the point where no part of the body may claim superiority or greater importance to the rest. Further, it demonstrates that humanity is an organically united body but with different parts.

A deeper understanding of the metaphor will show that there is one race of human beings but with different colors, some brown, some yellow, some red, some white and some black. In the absence of one color, the rest of humanity would continue to co-exist to extend the creation of God.

There is no literature more filled with metaphor and humor than the Bible. In the biblical narratives, written centuries ago, humor and metaphor are often used to express the meanings of the word of God. If the scripture is the word of God, which all of us Christians agree it is, then, God is humorous and metaphorical. In the light of the above assumptions, it is therefore necessary that we use some biblical examples to illustrate that our God is indeed humorous!

When God told Moses "to remove his shoes" before he approaches the burning bush, he was ultimately reminding him that before you near the presence of God, you must in humility remove the barriers and obstacles on your way that would prevent you from having a personal encounter with God. God was metaphorically telling Moses, "Come to me, the way you are created in humility and reverence, before you present yourself to the presence of God."

The burning bush experience is a metaphor which explains to us that in life one is transformed or changed forever. Moses was transformed and then empowered by the burning bush experience. "Remove your shoes" is a metaphor or humor which tells him how to enter a divine space, the divine presence, and before the mighty power of God. An invitation by God to Moses to be holy means for us the beginning of the universal invitation of all humanity to be holy. When God invites someone for a job, that person must undergo through a mysterious event such as that which Jesus underwent on the cross.

Moses was forever changed after the burning bush experience. He saw the bush burning, but the fire did not consume the bush. He heard the voice of God. For the first time, God revealed his name "Yahweh" as the being who lives eternally. One cannot hear the voice of God and know his name and remain the same. You must be changed and transfigured spiritually. The revelation of God to Moses was a gift to the people of Israel and a gift to the world. This gift was couched in the language of humor and metaphor which indicates the deeper level of how God wants to love and communicate with humanity.

Again, when the Prophet Jeremiah says that God "duped him," he was expressing his emotional state of anger against God. Jeremiah was sad and disappointed. Jeremiah in his humanity resisted God's invitation to go and proclaim to the chosen people about the impending danger. God sent him to the stiff-necked, recalcitrant, belligerent, and stubborn people. Initially, Jeremiah refused to go, but God insisted that he must go, and in doing so he experienced another "burning bush" and met the infidelity and wickedness of his own people. He experienced their belligerency. But God was with Jeremiah in his work of service to the people.

When God invites someone for service, he uses the person for a divine purpose and calls one unconditionally. You may find yourself unworthy, but God would think otherwise. The word "duped" is a metaphor and humor to illustrate that God is all knowing. He uses the smart way to invite people into action, and wherever we see human resistance, we also witness God's insistence and firmness. When someone says, "I cannot do it," God will say, "You must do it."

When Jesus tells Peter the Apostle, "Get behind me, Satan," he was not intending to demean or derogate him. On the contrary, he wants to tell Peter how little he knows about his mission and service, his sacrifice and the cross. Peter had earlier declared his faith by calling Jesus "the son of the living God" or "the Messiah" but later wished that Jesus would not suffer pain or death through the cross. Jesus tells Peter that the way of the cross is the best way to demonstrate divine service and save humanity. To serve means to go through the "burning bush," "the cross," and that will ultimately lead to salvation.

The way of the cross is the way to reach salvation. "Get behind me, Satan" is a way of saying to Peter, "You don't understand what service entails or what love means. It means the cross, sacrifice and passing through the burning bush and giving up one's life for the sake of many." The word Satan means "Obstacle." "EL DIABOLO" may be interpreted as any thing, idea, or person which is an obstacle for you to attain heaven or reach a goal in life. This is called Satan.

The power of humor in these episodes lies in the fact that Jesus called the first Pope "Satan," which means an obstacle. This means that any leader, civil or ecclesiastical, who cannot sacrifice his life in the service of others is not worth the name. He or She cannot take the role of a messenger, an Apostle, or a prophet of God.

When the father of John the Baptist received a message that the old woman Elizabeth would be pregnant and bear a son, Zachariah doubted the message of the angel of the Lord, but the angel said to him, "You will be silent until the child is born." Consequently, Zachariah remained mute until John the Baptist was born. Sometimes, when we doubt and resist God's intervention in our lives, we begin to realize that God's way is different from human way, and what humans may assume to be impossible, may turn out to be possible for God. The opposite of faith is doubt, and it is when Zachariah doubted the power of God that God showed his power by making him mute. Telling him to remain silent or speechless is a way of showing him to wait for the miracle of God to happen and in a way allowing him to experience his own type of "burning bush" and be changed forever.

God's own time is the best. When men and women say no, God says yes. When nature and science say it is impossible, God says it is possible. When men and women are silent, God is working, God is in action. When men and women talk and talk about what they see, and observe, God is busy fulfilling the purpose for which humanity is created. The silence of God is a metaphor used to describe his power through what is to happen. Thus, the last of the prophets came through the silence of Zachariah, and behind that silence was John the Baptist.

When Jonah was in the belly of the whale for "three days and three nights," it sounded unscientific and impracticable. But, before God, it was possible for Jonah to survive the ordeal of the heat and pain in the belly of the whale. Jonah survived not out of his own power, energy, or volition, but through the mighty power of God. "Belly of the whale" is a metaphor to demonstrate pain, sufferings, wounds, challenges or trials of all kinds, daily crosses, sorrows which many times are very excruciating for one to bear. "Belly of the whale" could also mean a passage from death to life. It is like the "burning of the bush" experience, the transformation experience, but it happened because God willed and used it to accomplish a desired task in Jonah.

Sometimes, we experience a situation like being in the belly of the whale when we are at a crossroads in our lives and unable to make decisions or the right choices. A situation can be so challenging that one needs to die severally or fail severally before one can succeed. How many times did Abraham Lincoln fail before he became the president of the United States? How many times did Joe Biden fail to become the President? How many times did Jesus fall on the cross? How Jonah survived the three days agony has been allegorically compared to the three days of our Lord in the tomb. But Our Lord conquered death to save us and to reassure those who believe in him to equally conquer death to have life. Victory is won through the cross and sacrifice, and that is the essence of Christian life.

When Jesus told his disciples "to beware of the leaven of the Pharisee and Sadducees," they thought that Jesus meant "bread." They were short of bread themselves, and Jesus reminded them of the miracles of the multiplication of bread on two occasions, but they still believed that it was bread to which Jesus was referring. The leaven of the Pharisees and Sadducees meant their doctrine and behavior, which is opposite to the Christian way of life. The Pharisees and Sadducees taught men and women to obey the laws of Moses but were the last people to practice what they teach. Jesus called them hypocrites because what they teach is different from what they do.

There are many of us who are bi-polar personality Christians, who hear one thing on Sunday morning, and do the exact opposite at home. There are many Christians who live double lives and do exactly like the Pharisees and the Sadducees. The metaphor "leaven" means things, ideas, and persons which are false. It means false teachers, prophets, pastors, and priests of our own time who spread false teaching, preaching prosperity without the cross and doing all kinds of false miracles, incantations, and magic in the name of Jesus, but their real life at home is quite different. Rabindranath Tagore wrote around the year 1913 about these kind of Christians,

> "Go not to the temple to put flowers upon the feet of God, first fill your own house with fragrance of love and kindness; Go not to the temple to light candles before the altar of God, first remove the darkness of sin, pride and ego from your heart; Go not to the temple to bow down your head in prayer, first learn to bow in humility before your fellow men and apologize to those you have wronged. Go not to the temple to pray on bent knees, first bend down to lift someone who is downtrodden. And strengthen the young ones, not crush them. Go not to the temple to ask for forgiveness for your sins, first forgive from your heart, those who hurt you."

It is important to say something detailed about the Pharisees and the Sadducees. These two sets of people were enemies of Jesus, and sometimes enemies to themselves. They had different doctrines. The Pharisees were a religious body with no political ambition. The Sadducees on the other hand were the priestly and aristocratic class, wealthy and not ready to forfeit their job, their comfort, and their place in the society. The Pharisees accepted the scripture and all other Jewish traditions. The Sadducees only accepted the written law of Moses. The Pharisees believed in the resurrection of the dead, angels, and spirits. The Sadducees did not believe in the resurrection. The Pharisees believed in fate/providence; the Sadducees believed in unrestricted free will. The Pharisees believed in the coming of the Messiah, but the Sadducees did not, believing that the idea of the Messiah was fake.

When Jesus claimed that He was "the resurrection and the life," that was a powerful metaphor to teach about "life after death." We believe that our God is the God of the living and not the dead. The God of Abraham, Jacob, and Isaac is a living God. The belief in the "after-life" is a long held Christian belief. Jesus believed it when he said, "I will go to the Father," and in another place he said, "In my father's house there are many mansions" Again, he told the repentant thief crucified with him, "Today you shall be with me in Paradise." Jesus emphatically says that whoever believes that he is the resurrection and life will never die, and those who died believing in him shall rise again.

What is life? The life that is meaningful is the life with and in Jesus. Without the life in Jesus, we appear dead, existing, but not living. There are four types of death—physical death, when the vital signs are no longer functioning; emotional death, when there are no more feelings of joy and happiness in the heart; moral death, when one cannot differentiate between the good and bad, light and darkness, truth and falsehood; and spiritual death, when there is no sense of God in the human spirit. The last one is the worse type of death. But only the grace of God can bring us back to life again. If we have experienced any of such types of death, then our God is the God of those who believe in him, hope in him, and die loving him. Without God in our lives, life itself is meaningless, not purposeful, and useless. Men and women created in "God's image and likeness" belong to God, and our final home is God's home that we call Eternity.

Enjoy this brief humor!!

"After every long and boring sermon, the parishioners filed out of the church saying nothing to the preacher. Toward the end of the line was a thoughtful person who always commented on the sermons. 'Pastor, today your sermon reminded me of the peace and love of God!' The Pastor was thrilled. No one had ever said anything like that about his preaching before. "Tell me why." "Well—it reminded me of the peace of God because it passed all understanding and the love of God because it endured forever!"

Lesson: If a preacher cannot explain his points in ten to fifteen minutes, he cannot do it in two hours!

When Jesus encountered the Samaritan woman at the well, he asked her of drinking water. The conversation gradually developed to the point where Jesus told her about her private life. She was shocked and she said, "Come, see a man who told me everything I have done." The Samaritan woman had an incredible experience with Jesus. That is exactly how revelation unfolds. She was completely changed and graduated from being an outcast to the primary disciple of Jesus. The woman at the well had the same encounter as Moses had at the "burning bush." Permit me to explore more deeply into this private conversation.

Privacy in the 21st century has become extremely expensive and explosive and sometimes untenable. In the past what was considered as a private life or privacy is no longer private. Many of the things we used to call private even at home or between friends are no longer private. The social media technology, internet, cyber-security outfits, public safety concerns, and bureau of intelligence have made public what we use to consider private. There is a lot of personal information of individuals on Facebook, Google, Instagram and websites that one would never have imagined in the past.

Suppose you meet a person you do not know, and you have not seen him before, and he tells you more about who you are, your finances, your relationships (good and bad), your background, your employment history, your private exploits, your habits and vices, your gossips, the number of times you have attempted suicide, and the number of times you have cheated your spouse, or your intent to commit murder, or how many times you have used drugs, the time and location of the event, or someone who tells you what you are planning in the next few days in committing fraud against your company, or your boss or the government. Such a person must be feared, respected as a prophet or superhuman person with extraordinary authority.

Sometimes, we have had the experience of the government coming very close to our personal freedom and liberty, especially when our personal privacy is compromised. But when Jesus tells us that he knows us through and through, he is not interfering with our personal freedom, or putting us to shame or ridicule, but making us believe that he is truly the Messiah, our God, our all and all in whom all our aspirations, desires, hopes and dreams should focus always. We should therefore empty our hearts, secrets, and privacy to him dwell for "he is our peace." As the musician Handel Messiah would sing, "I know that my redeemer lives," and when he comes, he will tell us everything as he told the "woman at the well." "I am he, the one speaking with you."

When Jesus cured the "ten lepers" and only one of them showed gratitude, he was also reminding us to be grateful for what we have and thank God for it, because very often we do not realize what we have until we lose it. "Leprosy" here is a metaphor representing all kinds of diseases including evil and sin. Leprosy is like aids, or coronavirus, which is highly contagious. In the time of Jesus, those who were inflicted with the disease of leprosy had bells hung around their necks or waists to indicate to the by-standers that lepers were approaching the place. Many would run away to avoid being infected by the disease.

When Jesus cured the ten lepers, he instructed them to show themselves to the priest as a witness to the cure. Some of these diseases were also attributed to demons and curing them would mean removing the demons responsible. Only the priests could certify that such diseases had been eliminated. As the "ten lepers" went away rejoicing about the incident, one of them came back to Jesus to give thanks. He happened to be a Samaritan. Jews and Samaritans did not get along, but one can observe that during a crisis of ill-health, a common misfortune had broken down their national barriers. The lepers had one thing in common—they needed help.

A common need can bring the world together. The whole world needed a vaccine because of the coronavirus that besieged the universe. Most importantly, the whole world needs God who guided and directed the scientists to manufacture the essential vaccine for the cure of the disease. The lepers needed God, and that common need can demolish isolation, discrimination, racism, bigotry, and prejudice. When the lepers, were on their way, one of them looked at himself, saw the difference in his body, and came back to Jesus to give thanks. The rest went their way. This also shows the human condition—once, a man gets what he wants, he never comes back. This is true of all of us. The one who came back was cured and healed. He was healed because he appreciated the work of God in him. Healing so touched his soul and heart that he needed to come back to say, "Thank you Jesus." Sometimes, we are ungrateful to our parents who cared for us, for so many years; we are ungrateful to our fellow-men and women, friends, teachers, doctors, priests, police, and significant others who contributed to our well-being and lifted us up when we were down. The tragedy is that we take it for granted and often we do not even say thank you.

"Leper" as a metaphor means "sinners" – "All we like sheep have gone astray" as the psalmist would say. Like sinners we often do not want to show gratitude to God for what he is doing in our lives. When things are out of shape, we run to him and after that, we forget God. This is a sad human condition—ingratitude. My question is this, "How many of us say prayers before and after meals? How many do so as they go to bed? How many say to their mothers, "Thanks, Mummy, for your wonderful care" or to the dad, "Love you, Daddy". It is said that "he who gives thanks receives double gifts from God."

When Jesus said, "I have come to set the earth on fire" and "how I wish it were already blazing," he was using a powerful metaphor to teach us that his coming to the world would bring a challenge to the society in so many shapes and forms. Stories about how families have been torn apart because of religious beliefs abound. There are many experiences about how religious wars were fought in the past. There are various sad memories of the "dark ages," the time of the great inquisition, the French revolution, the reformation, and the counter-reformation. There are sad stories of how Catholics in some countries were despised and discriminated against because of their faith. Wars have been fought because of religious differences, but in the 21st century there are still divisions and acrimony in some quarters.

We have come a long way thanks to ecumenical dialogue and interreligious communications, yet there are conflicts and divisions. There are obvious divisions among Jews and non-Jews, between Christians and non-Christians, and between Catholics and non-Catholics. So, what Jesus is saying about "fire on earth" is true. In context, he is saying that his coming will usher in a challenge to all believers and their normal way of life. The coming of the kingdom will challenge the family units, the communities, and the nations. In the 21st century, there are varieties of religious experiences. Families do have some of their members who do not believe in God (atheists) some who doubt what God is doing in their lives (agnostics), some who believe in so many divine beings (pagans or polytheists), some who are Christians but are no longer practicing their faith (fallen Christians) and some who "faith-cross" from one religion to another (dysfunctional Christians).

A parent came to me one day and complained that the daughter does not believe in God anymore but in demons. I was shocked to hear that from such a wonderful Christian family. There are many families who struggle with this challenge every day. How do you feel when your daughter or child does not go to the same Church as you do? When my sister-in-law left the Catholic Church and joined another denominational Church, I felt bad. The stories go on and on. What Jesus is saying by "setting fire on earth" is that his coming will bring a moment when individual responsibility will matter a lot. Each person will make his or her own decision about life and death. "You are for him or against him." In other words, when someone is with him, and in him, and for him (*per ipsum, et cum ipso, et in ipso*), then, and only then, can he or she be known as a true disciple. Jesus is saying the faith one professes must be possessed in action and in truth. The worst thing that can happen to the person who believes is to be indifferent or silent!

The test of love is obedience. There are those who protest their love in words, but who at the same time bring pain and heartbreak to those whom they claim to love. There are children and young people who say that they love their parents yet cause them grief and anxiety all the time. There are husbands who say they love their wives, and wives who say, they love their husbands, and who, yet by their attitude and insensitivity, irritability and unkindness, bring pain to one another. To obey, we need help from the Holy Spirit, who is the bringer of love. As we often say, "Lord, send us your Spirit, ….and enkindle in us the fire of your love, so that the earth will be renewed." The Holy Spirit helps us deal with our fears and hidden agenda. He helps us deal with our doubts about ourselves and our environment.

He helps us deal with our differences, ideologies, and tendencies that cause barriers between us and God. The Holy Spirit helps us deal with our "inner space" of life to make godly decisions and right choices. St Augustine was quoted as saying, "Love not well-shared is not well-possessed." So, love is shared and possessed through obedience.

Another test of love is sacrifice and suffering. Listen to this story culled from an anonymous author. "One night a man had a dream. He dreamed he was walking along the beach with the Lord. Across the sky flashed scenes from his life. For each scene, he noticed two sets of footprints in the sand. One belonged to him and the other to the Lord. When the last scene of his life flashed before him, he looked back at the footprints in the sand. He noticed that many times along the paths of his life, there was only one set of footprints. He also noticed that it happened at the very lowest and saddest times of his life. This really bothered him, and he questioned the Lord about it. "Lord, you said, once I decided to follow you, you'd walk with me always— all the way. But I have noticed that during the most troublesome times in my life, there is only one set of footprints. I don't understand why when I needed you most, you would leave me." The Lord replied,

"My precious child, I love you and I will never leave you. During your time of trial and suffering, when you see only one set of footprints, it was then that I carried you." When we believe that God is absent in our lives, especially in times of trials, we begin to think that he has abandoned us, but that is precisely when he is at work as God.

Another test of love is endurance and patience at God's own time. Listen again to this humor culled from the Church bulletin "jokes of the day."

An old preacher was dying. He sent a message to his doctor and his lawyer, both church members, to come to his home. When they arrived, they were ushered up to the bedroom. As they entered the room, the preacher held out his hand and motioned for them to sit one on each side of the bed. The preacher grasped their hands, sighed contentedly, smiled, and stared at the ceiling. For a time, no one said anything. Both the doctor and the lawyer were touched and flattered that the preacher would ask them to be with him during his final moments. They were also puzzled. The preacher had never given them any indication that he particularly liked either of them. They both remembered his many long uncomfortable sermons about greed and avaricious behavior that made them squirm in their seats. Finally, the doctor said, "Preacher, why did you ask us to come?" The old preacher mustered up strength, then said, "Jesus died between two thieves, and that's how I want to go."

It might sound funny that the two visitors to the sick were seen as two thieves, but, paradoxically, one of the thieves received redemptions from the loving mercy of Jesus. "You will be in paradise with me today." It is in God's time that redemption comes, not in our own time or leisure. When God forgives, he does so with love and unconditionally. This story also teaches that for God, it is not too late to be saved or redeemed. Your entire struggle for salvation may end up in futility if you fail to continuously share the love of God in you with other people till the end of your life. Your misfortunes and disappointments in life can be turned into a blessing at the last minute, when you repent and convert to God with trust, convictions, and commitment. This is the paradox of life, and this is redemption in the full sense of the term.